TOKIN' T-REX
& HIS BUDDIES
Cannabis Coloring Book For Adults

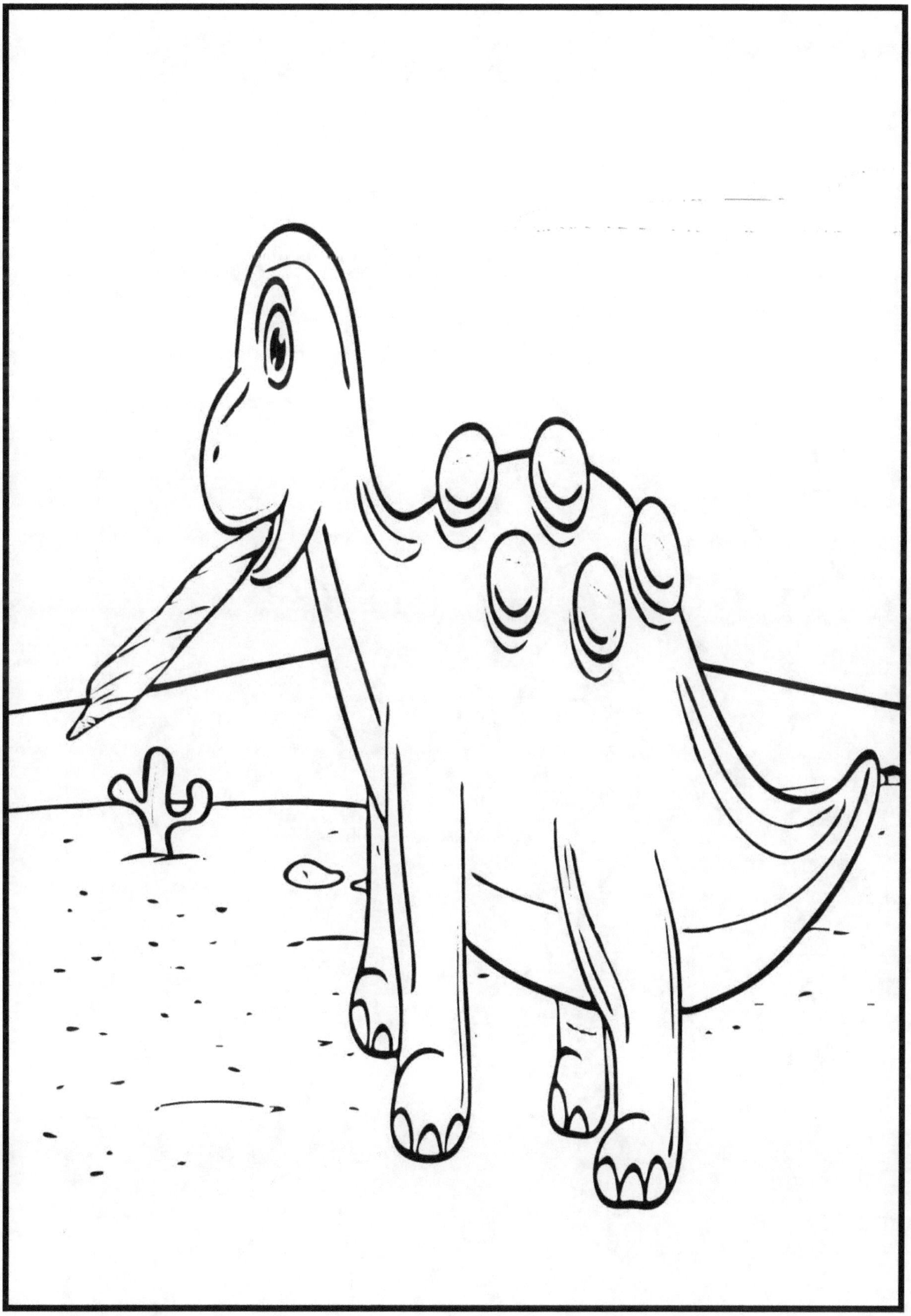

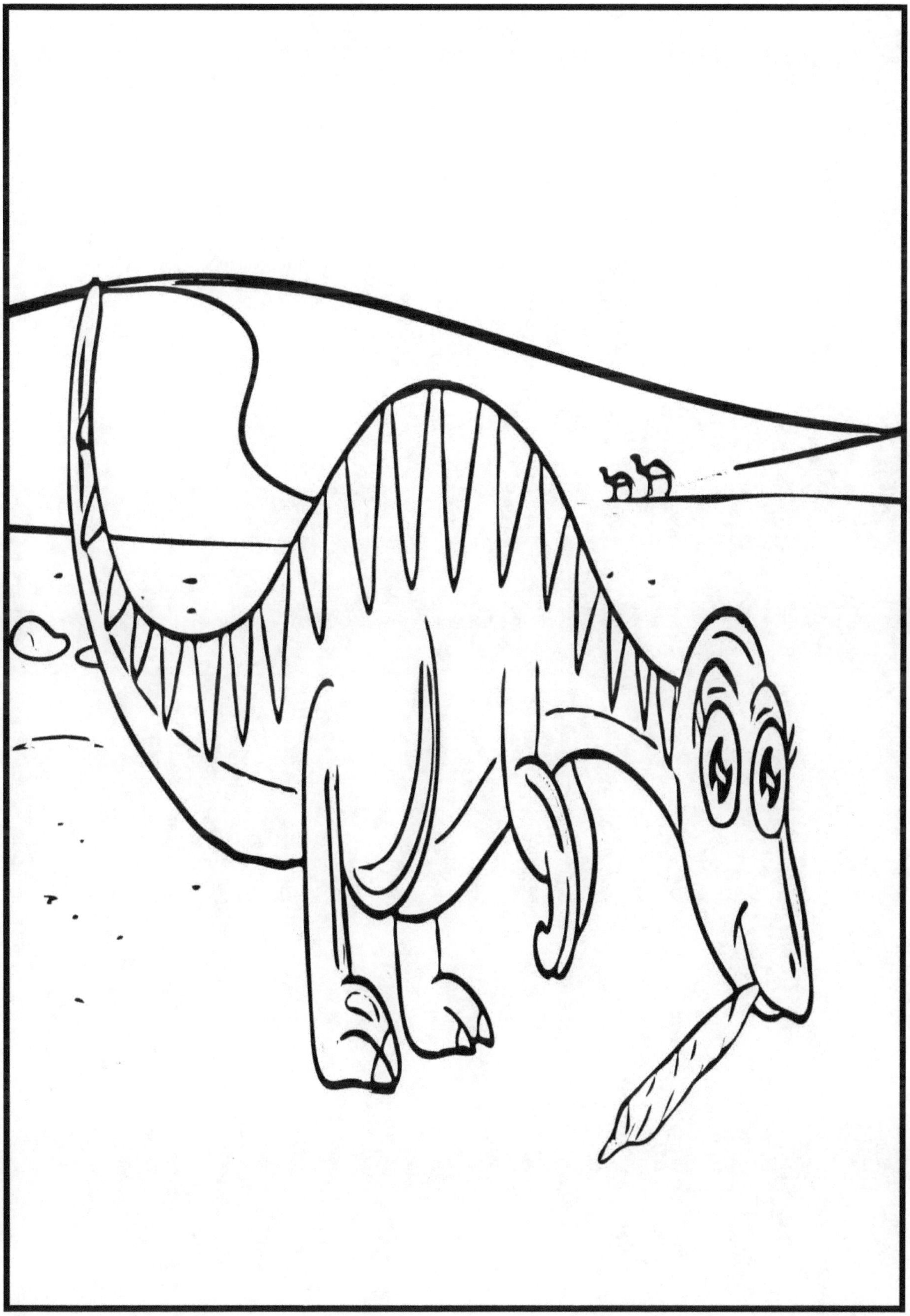

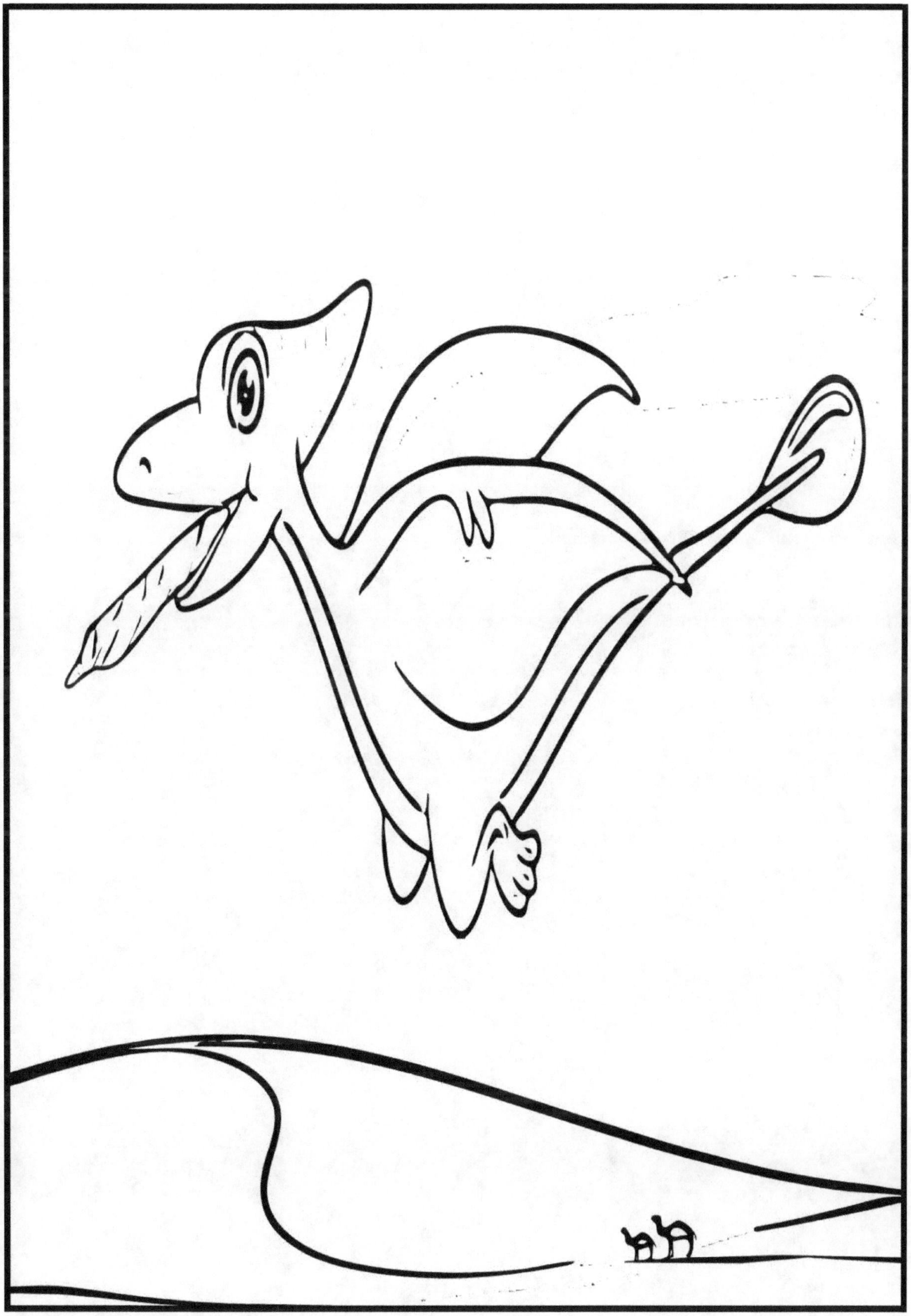

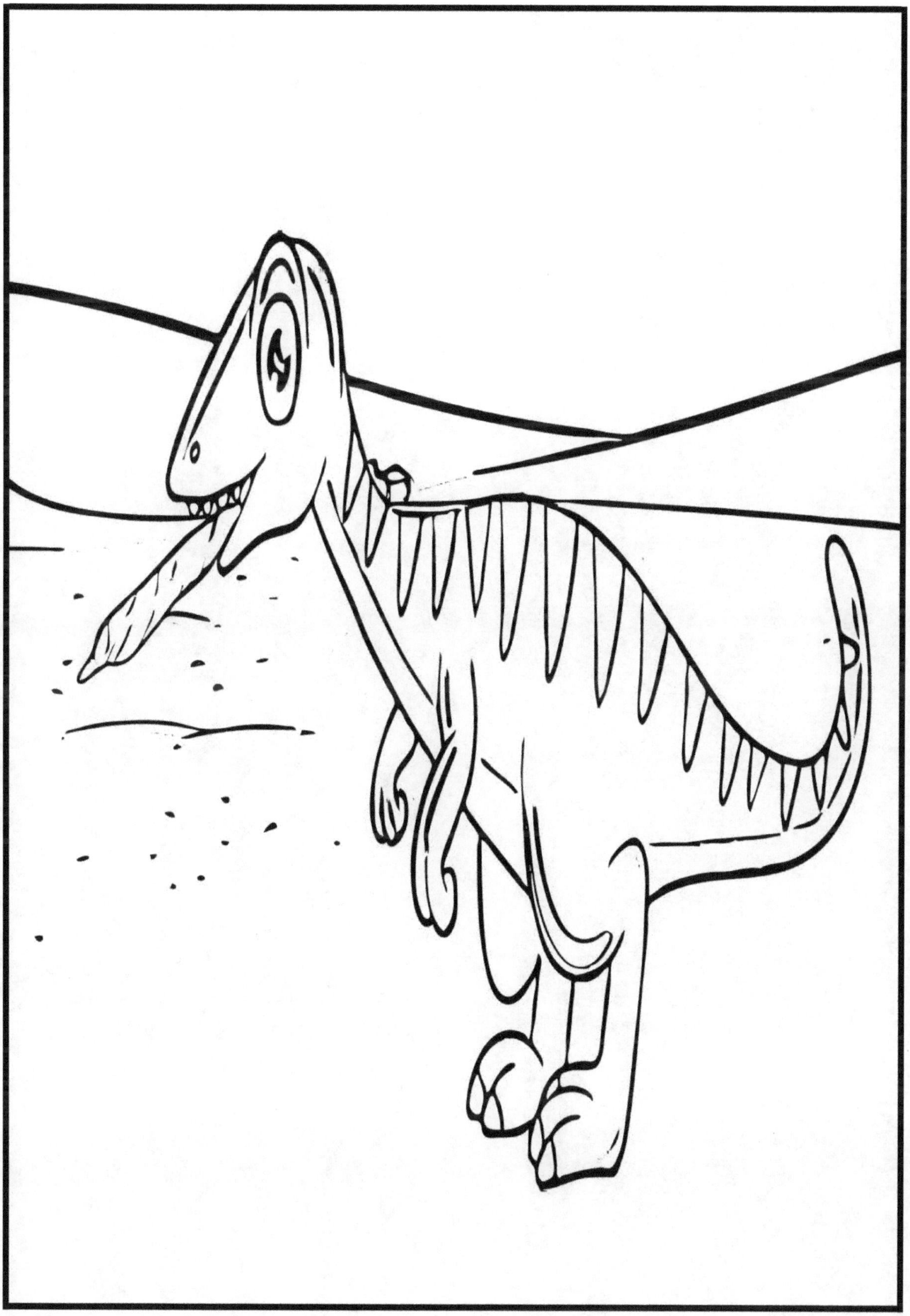

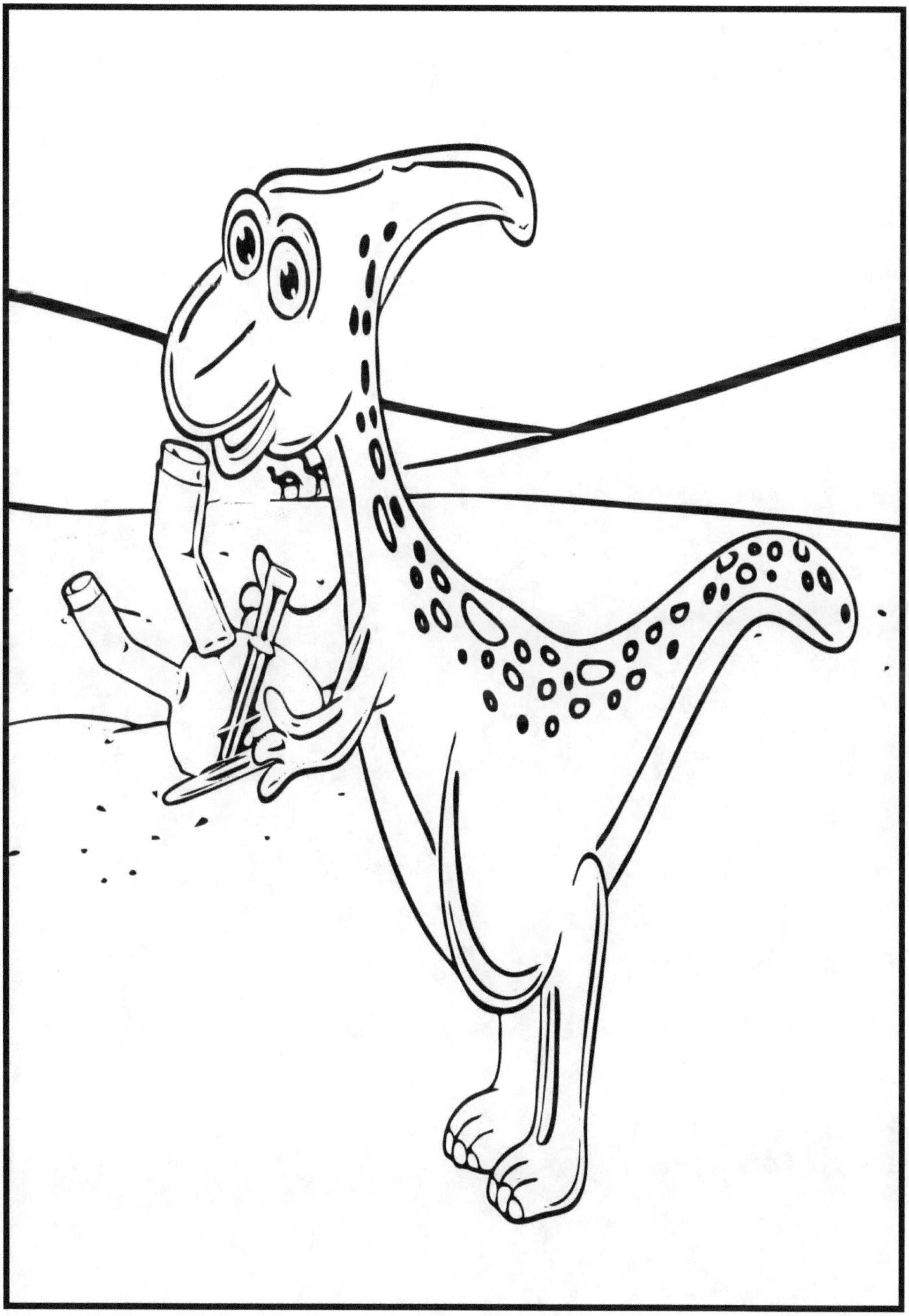

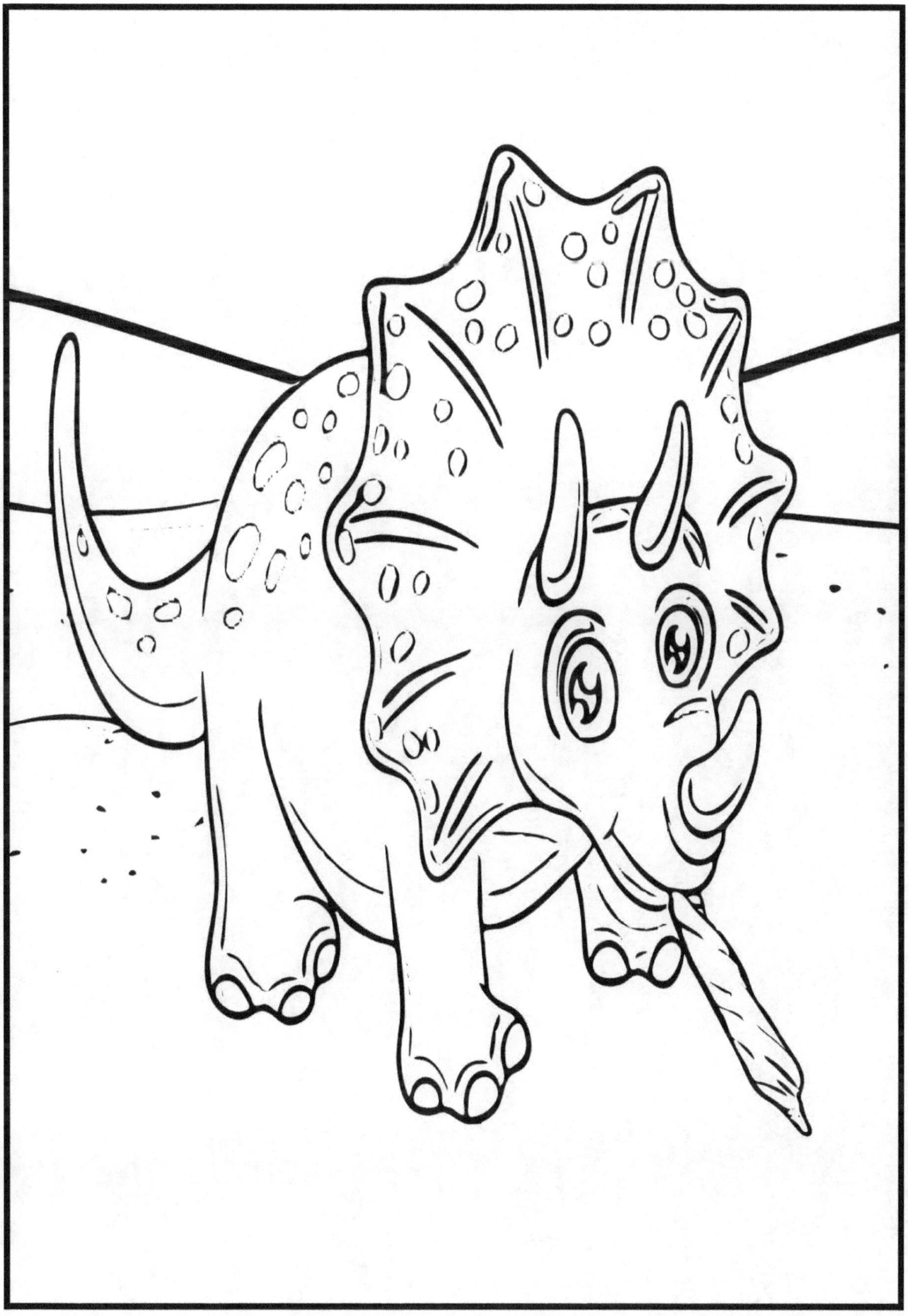

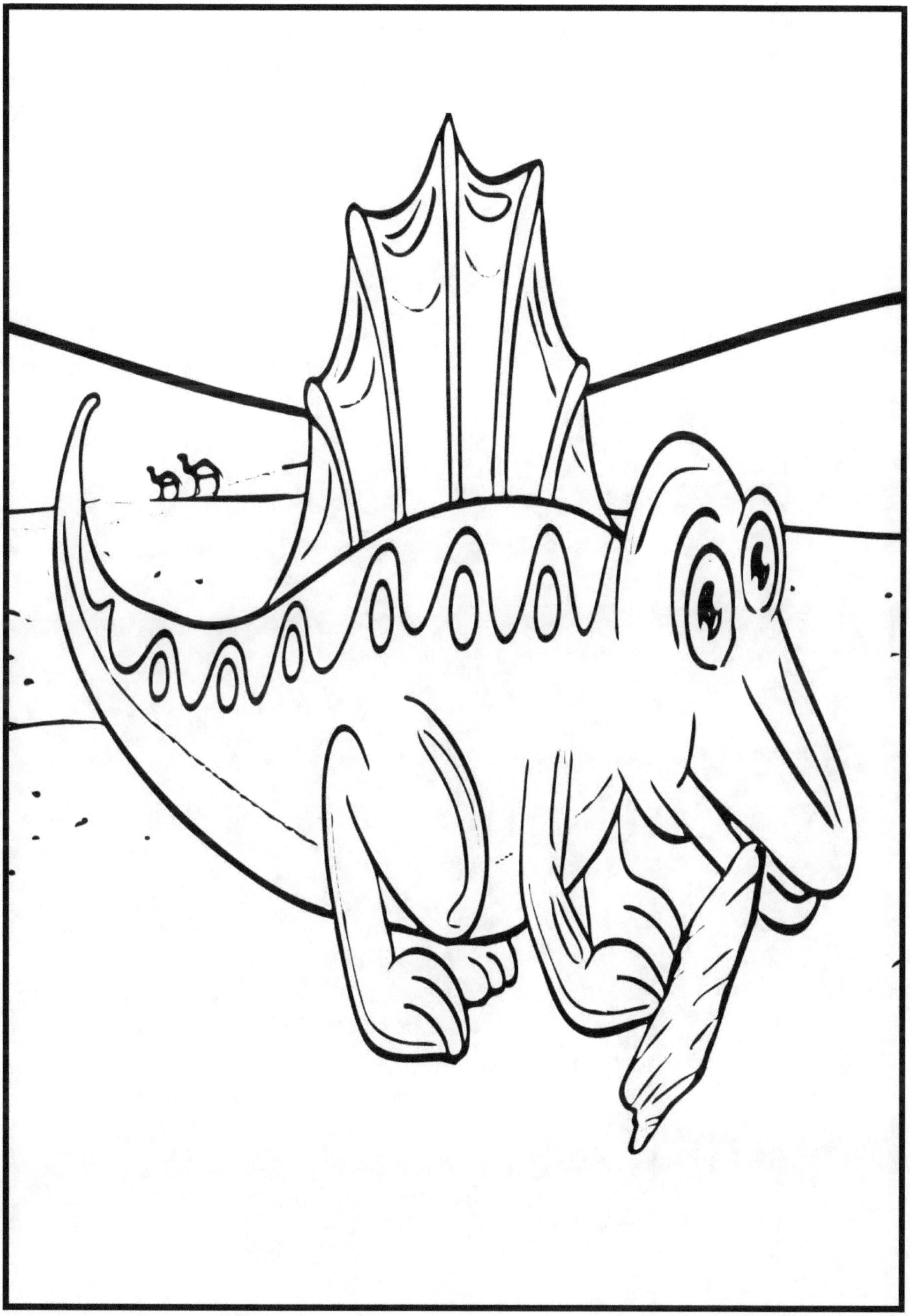

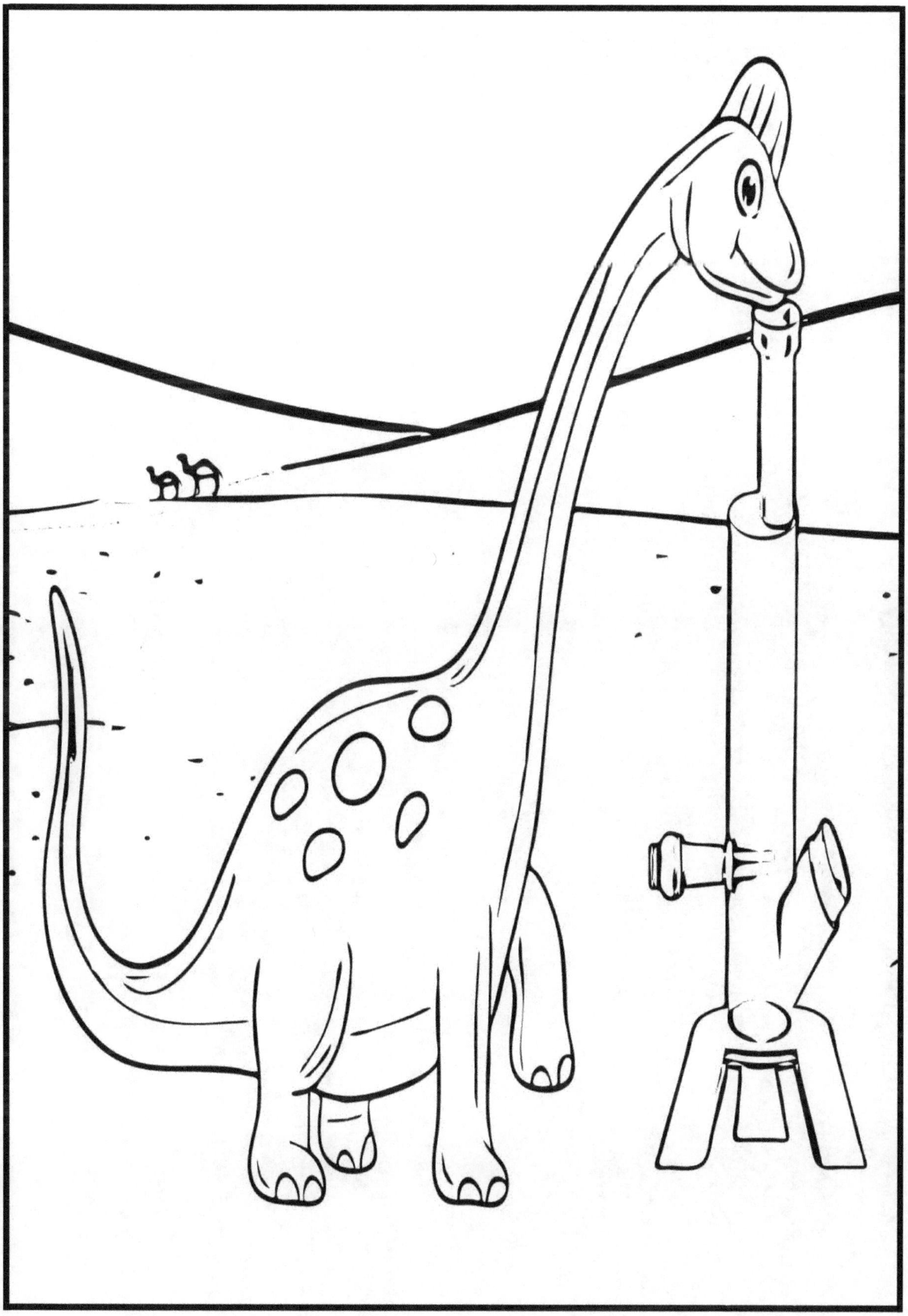

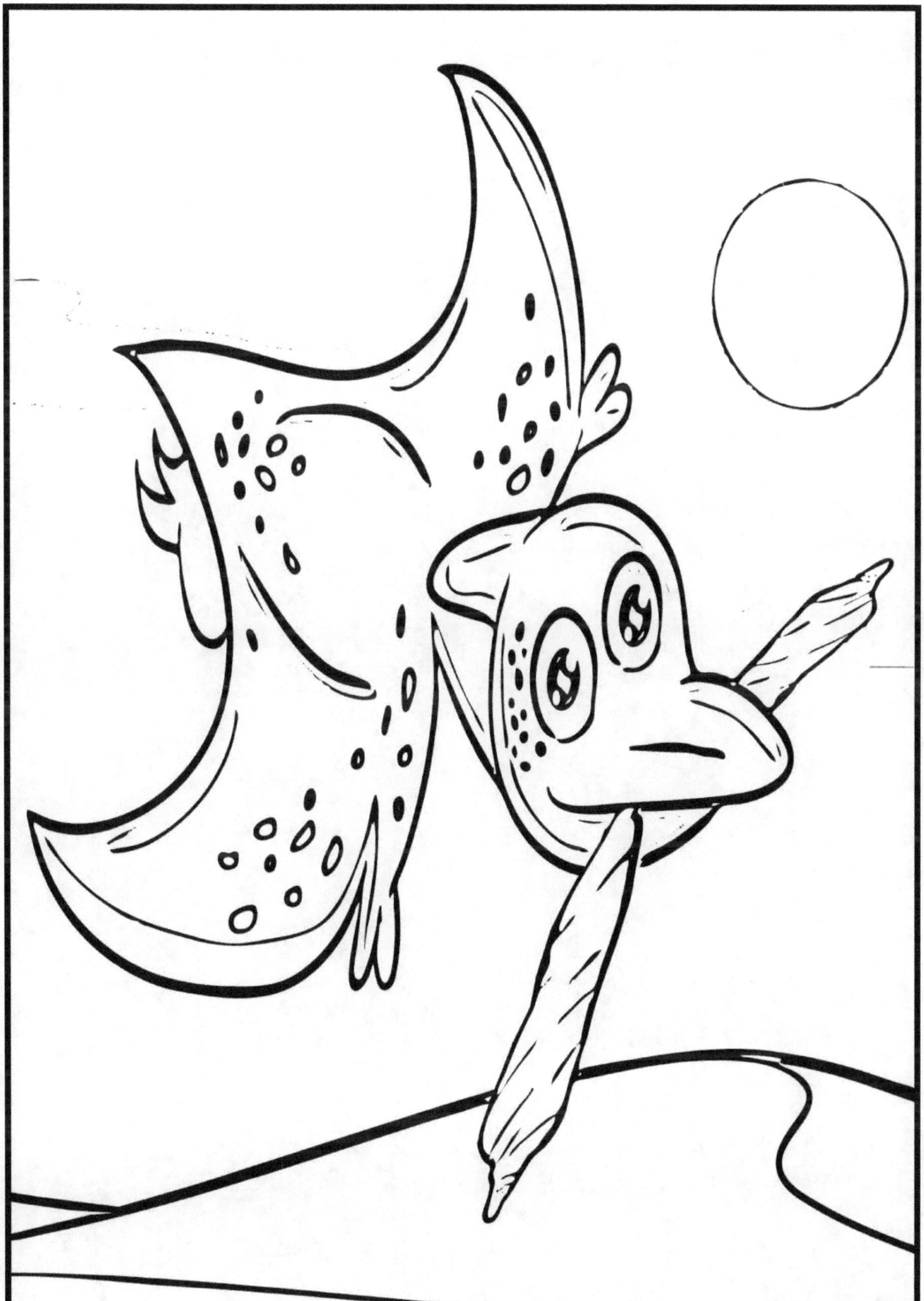

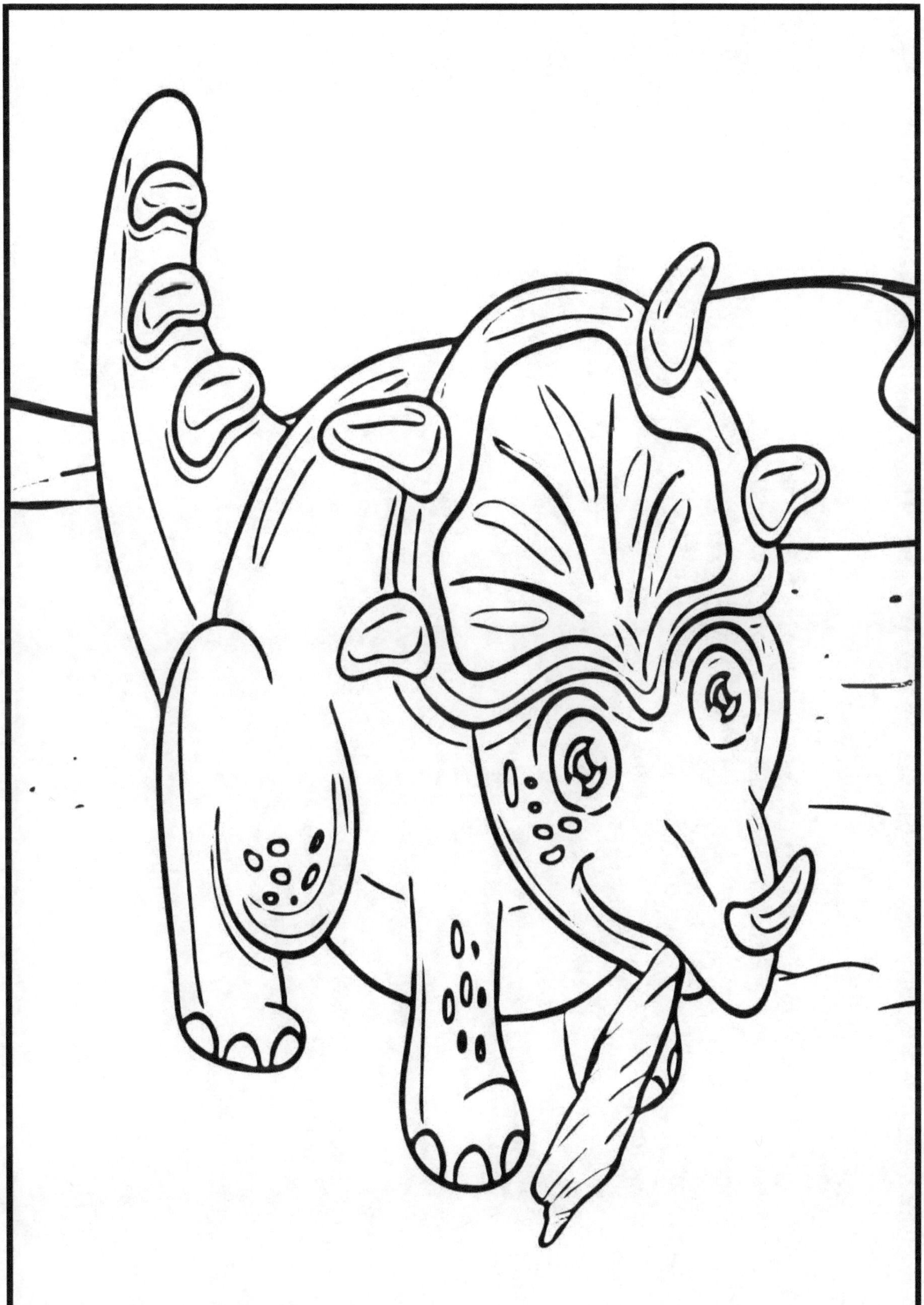

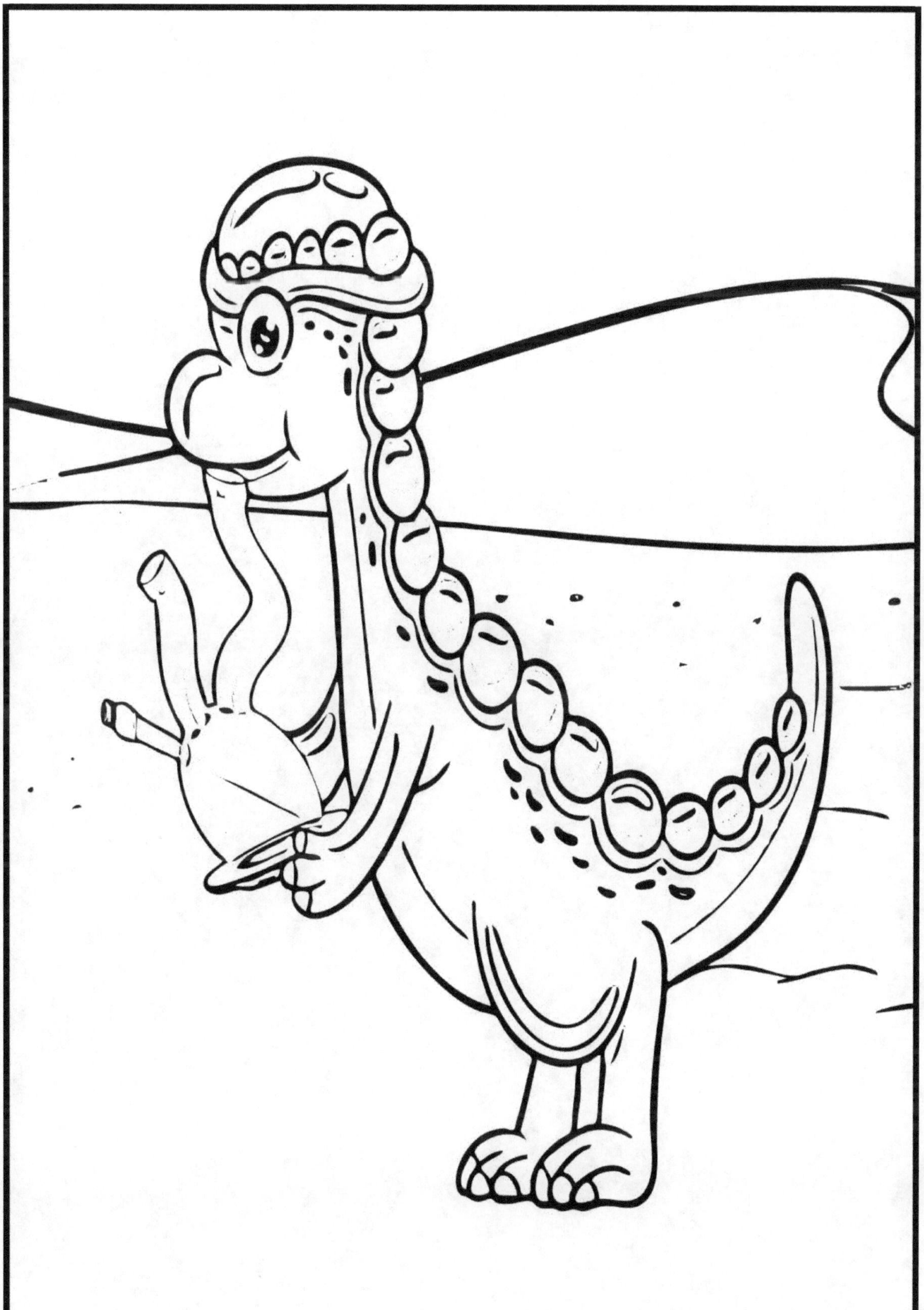

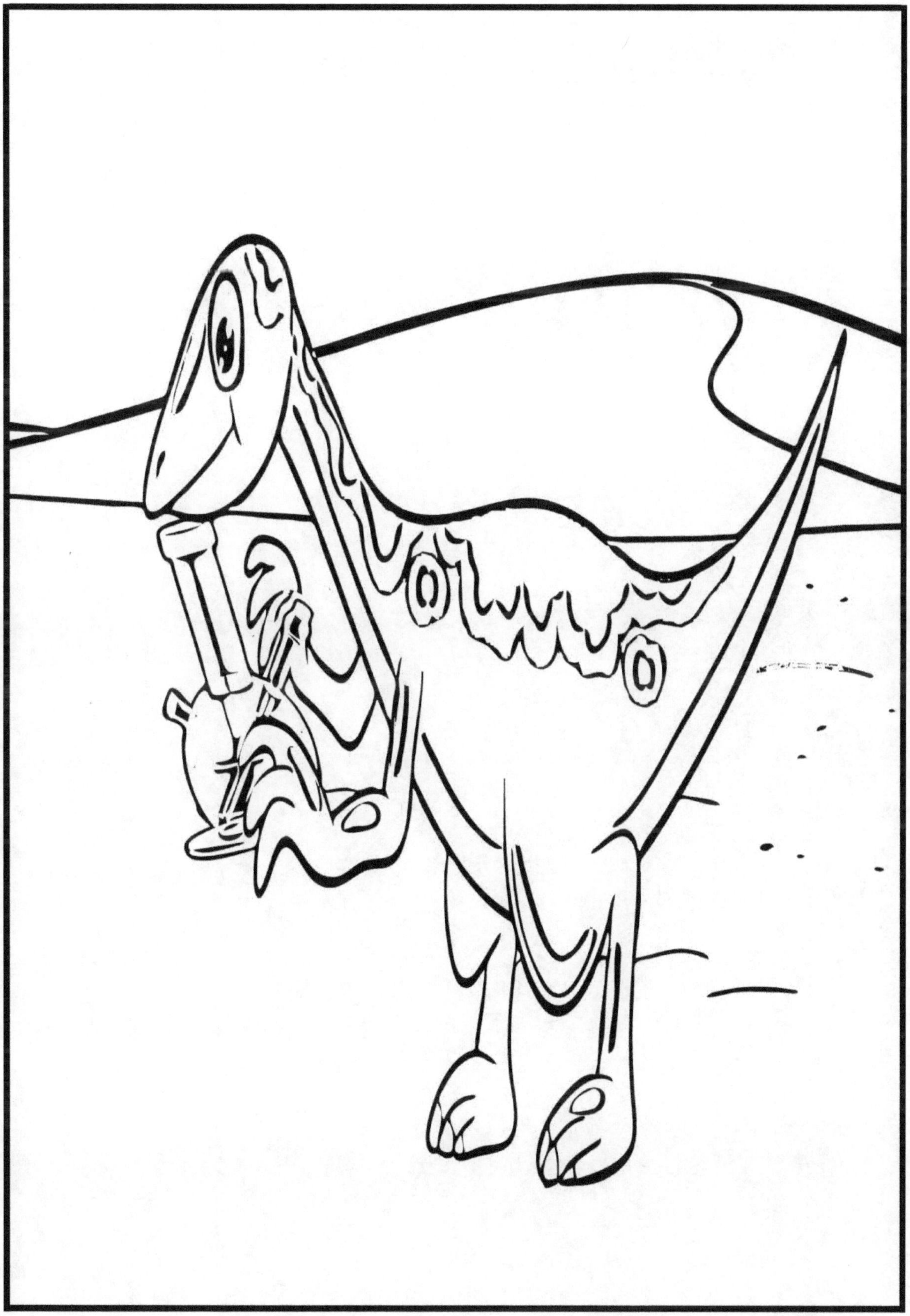

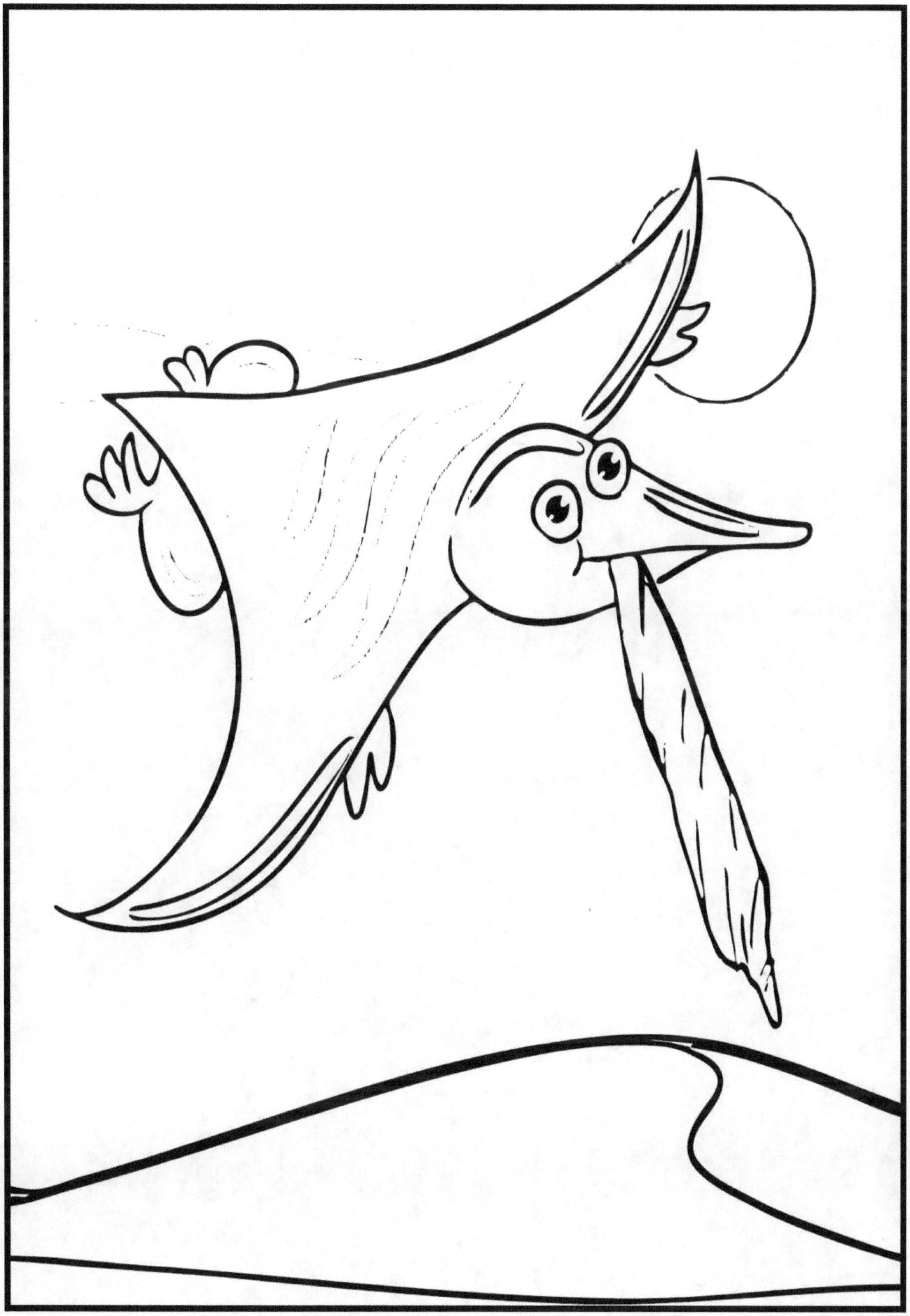

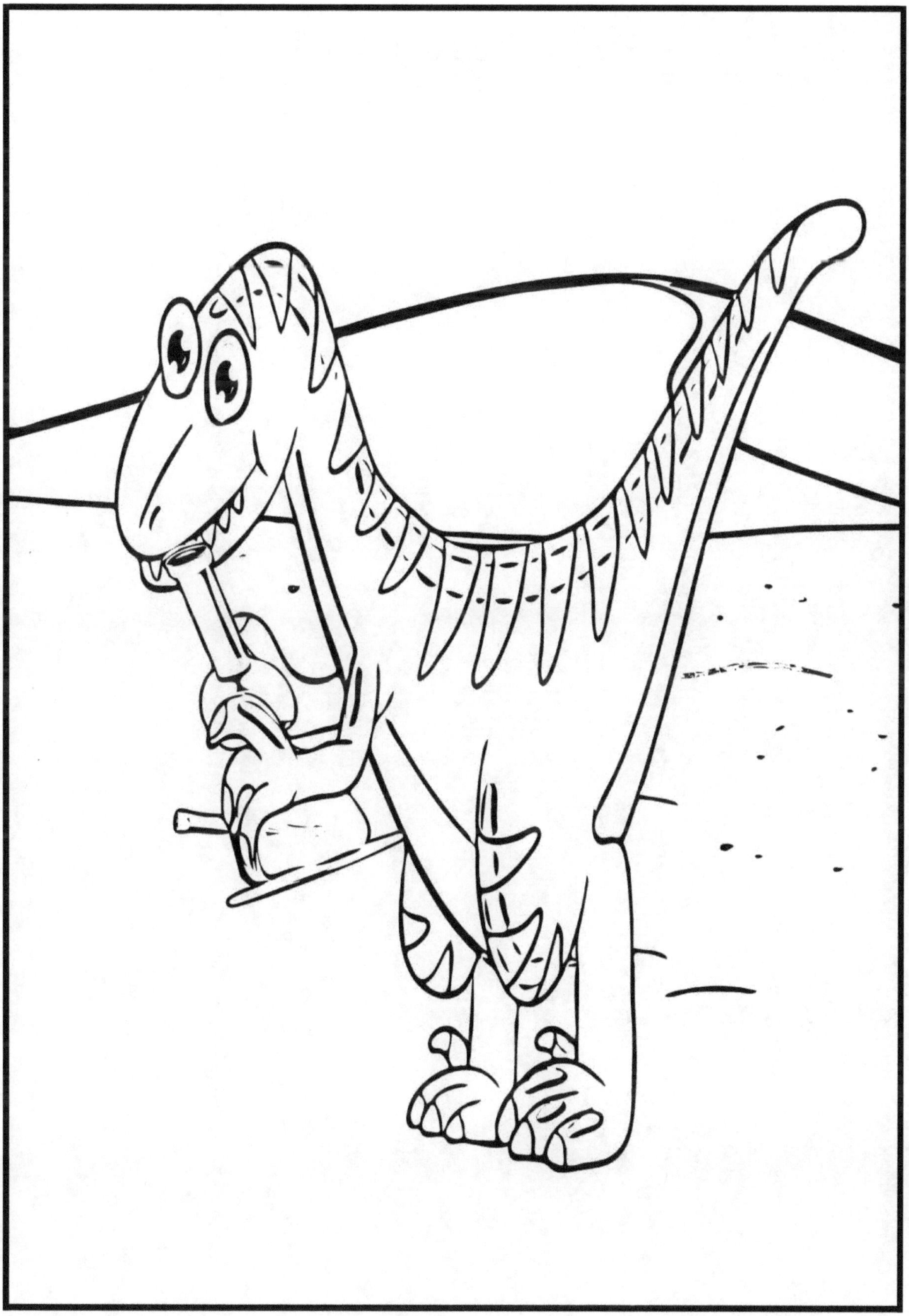

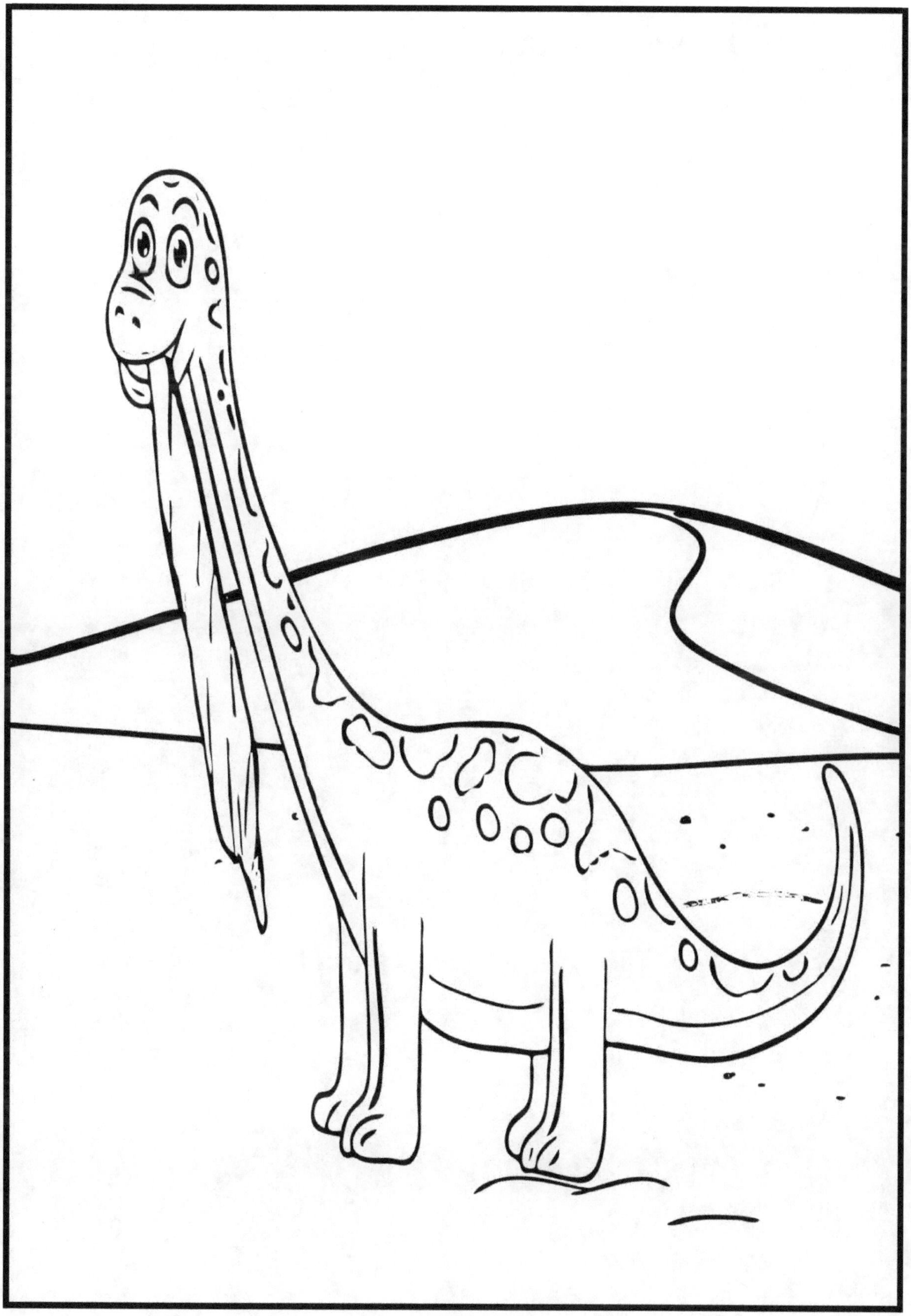

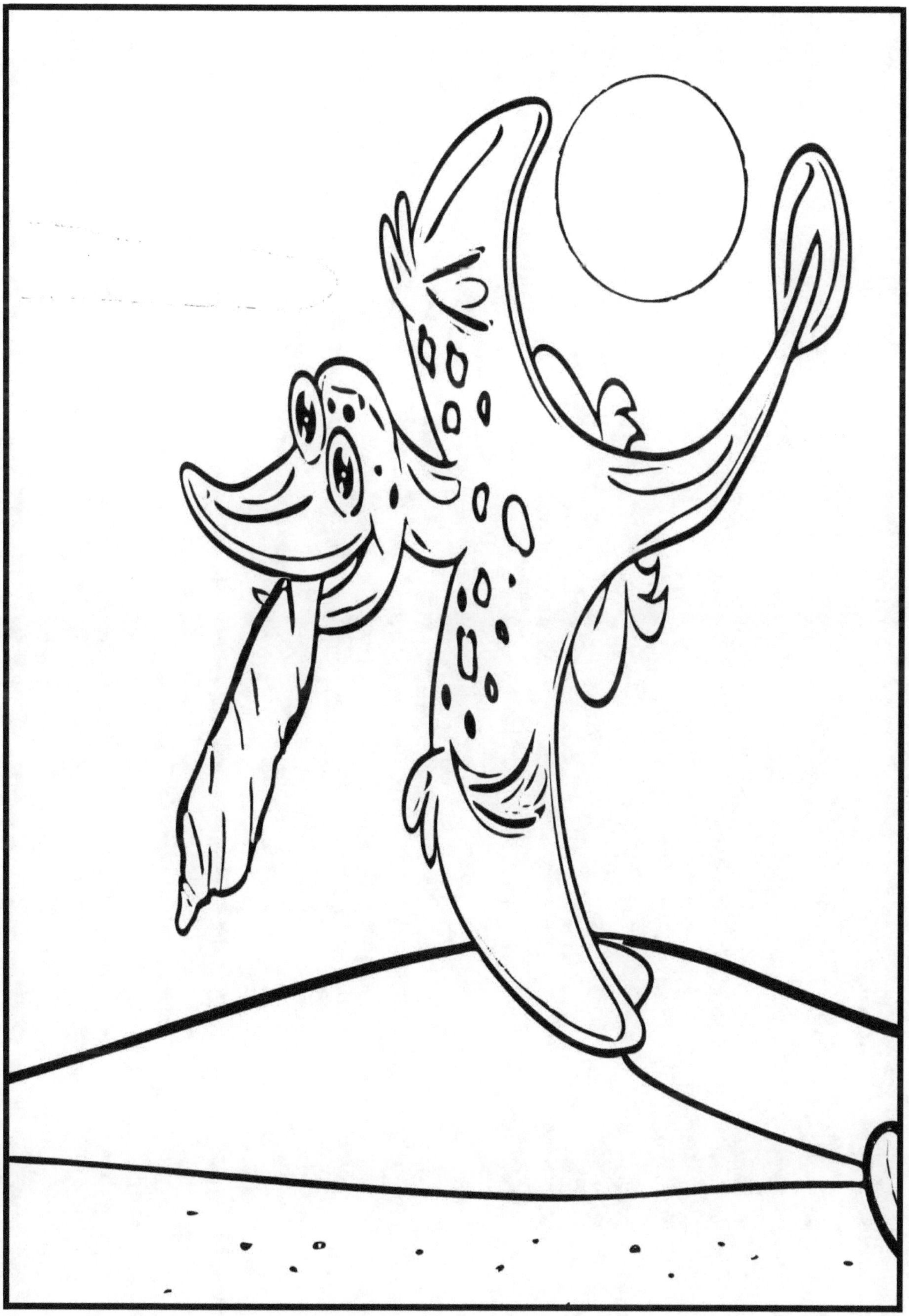

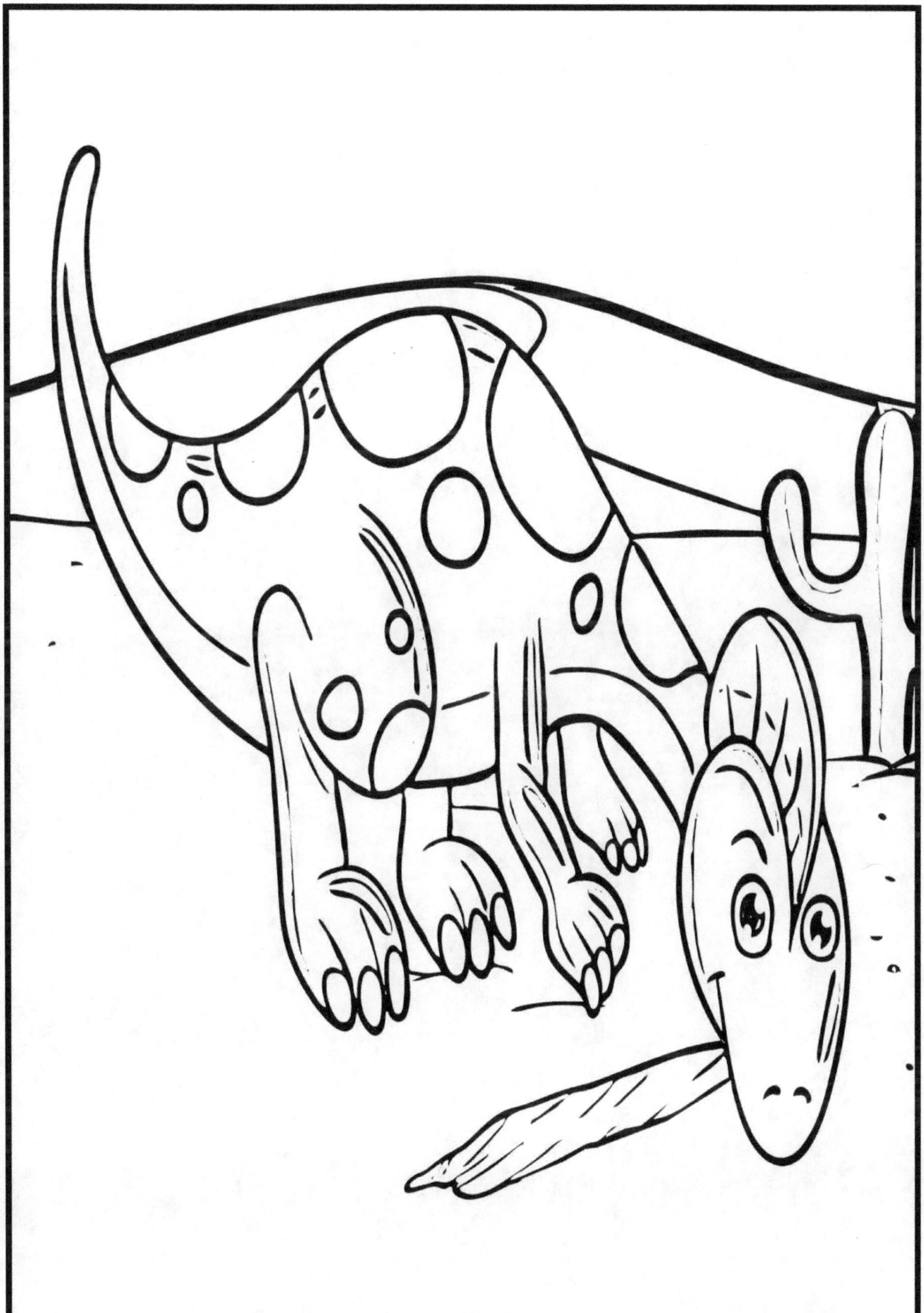

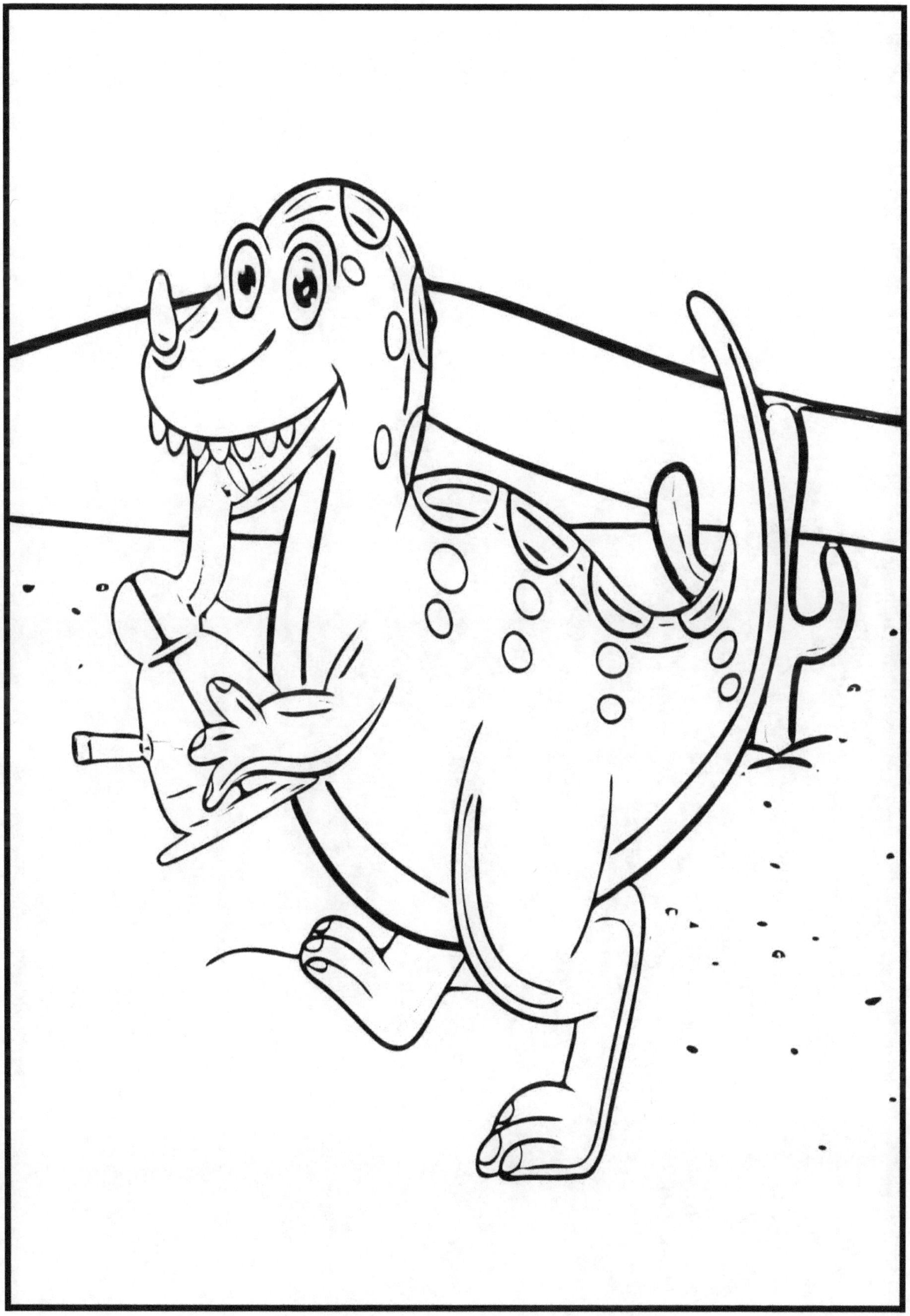

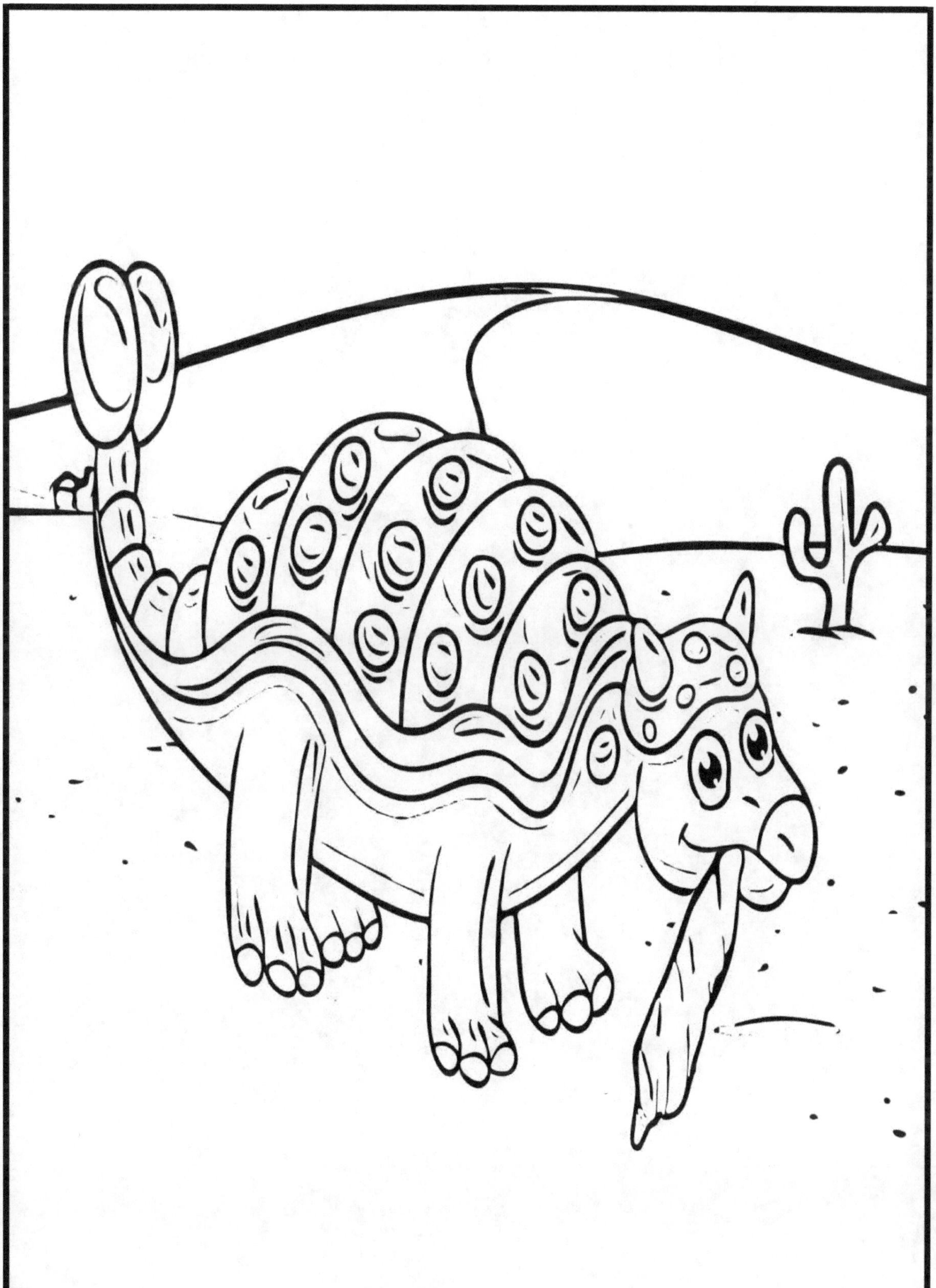

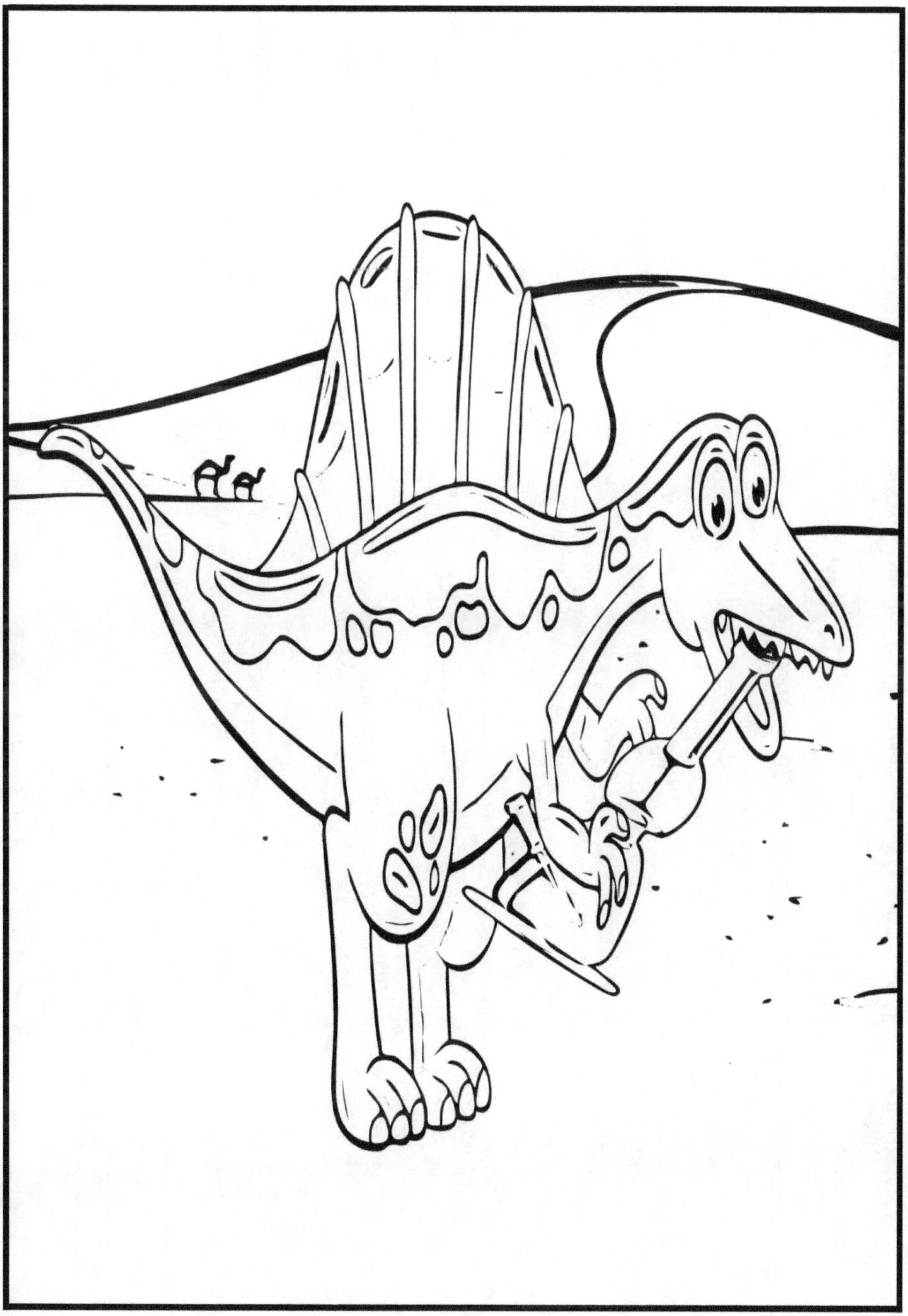

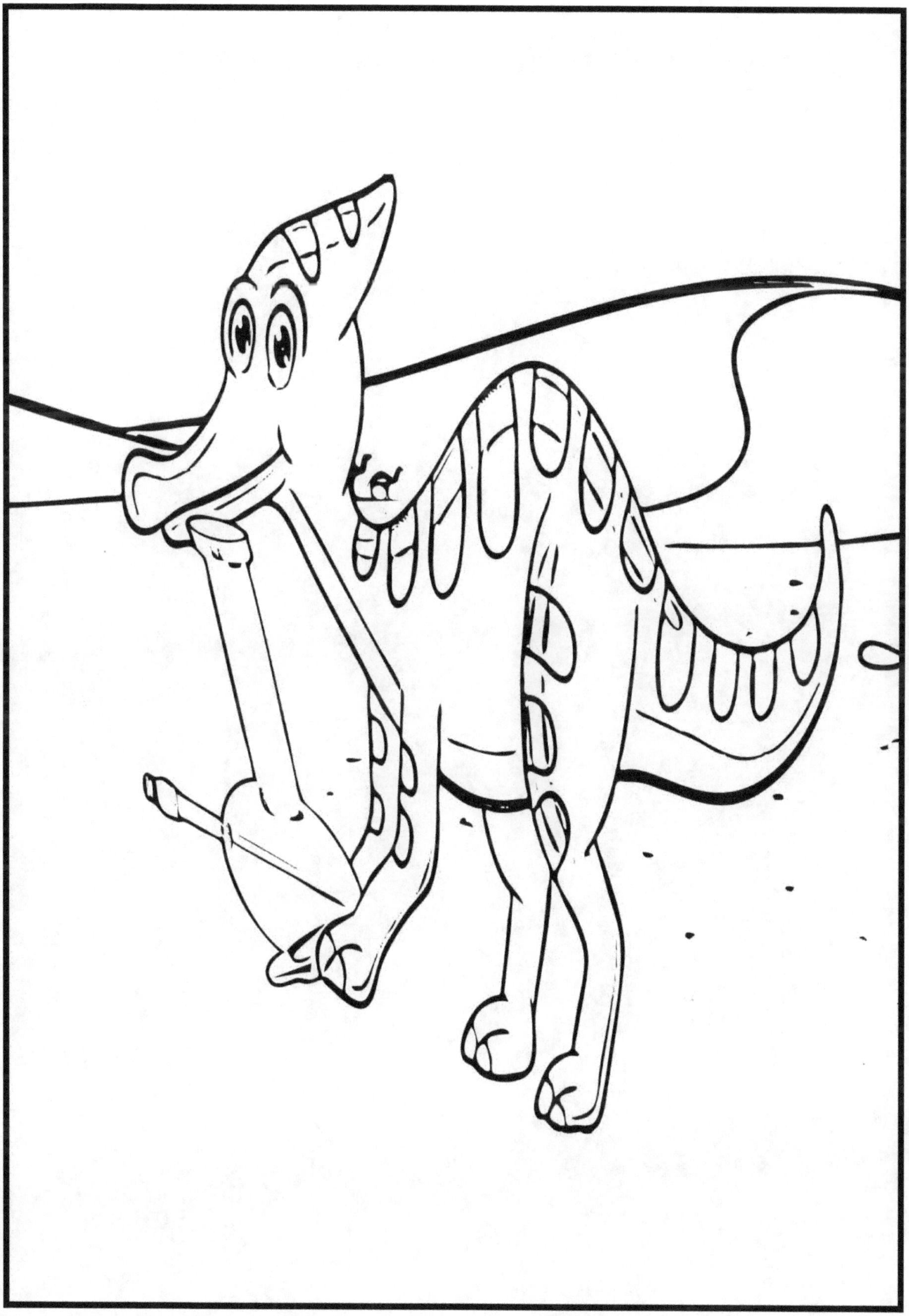

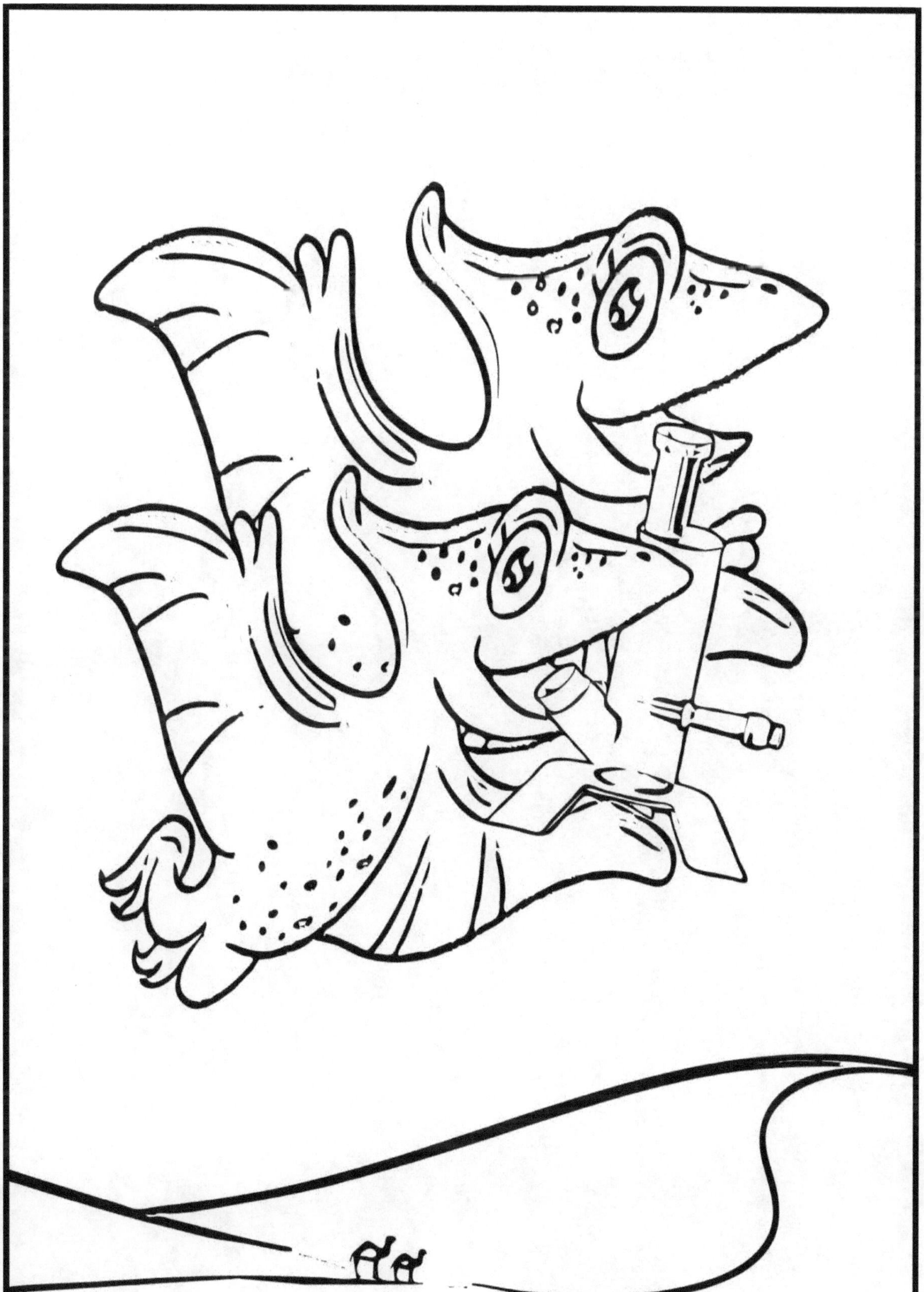

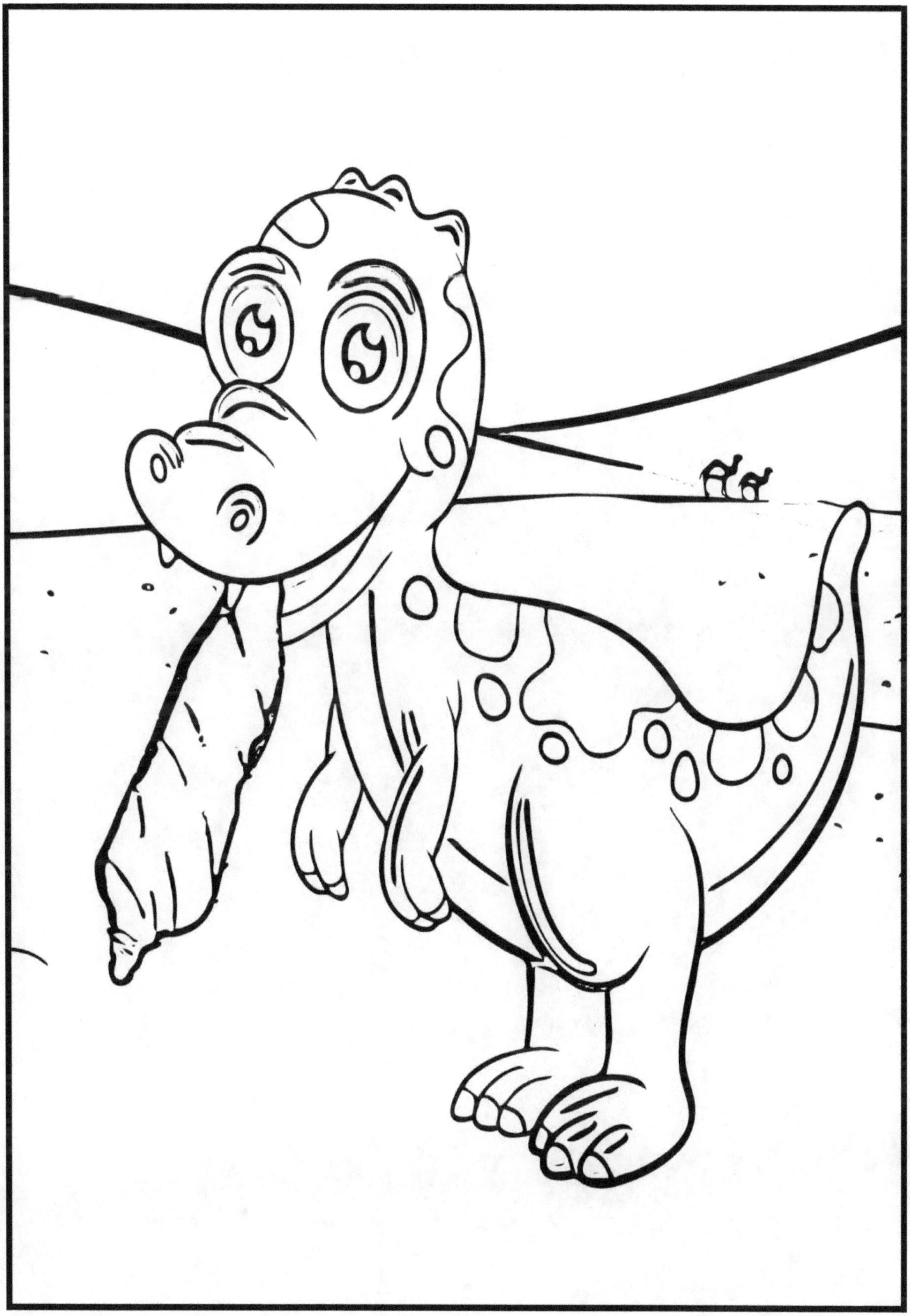

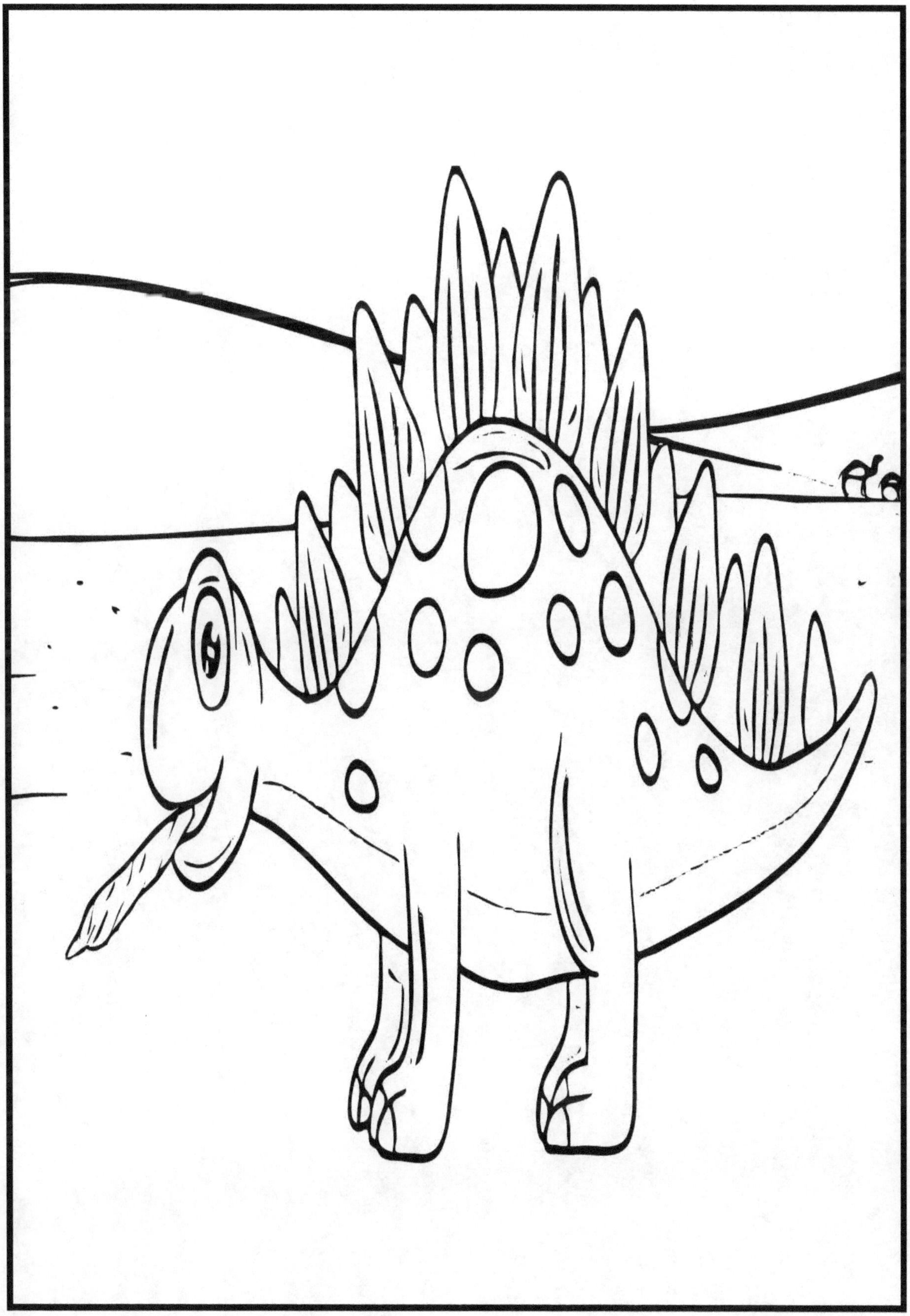

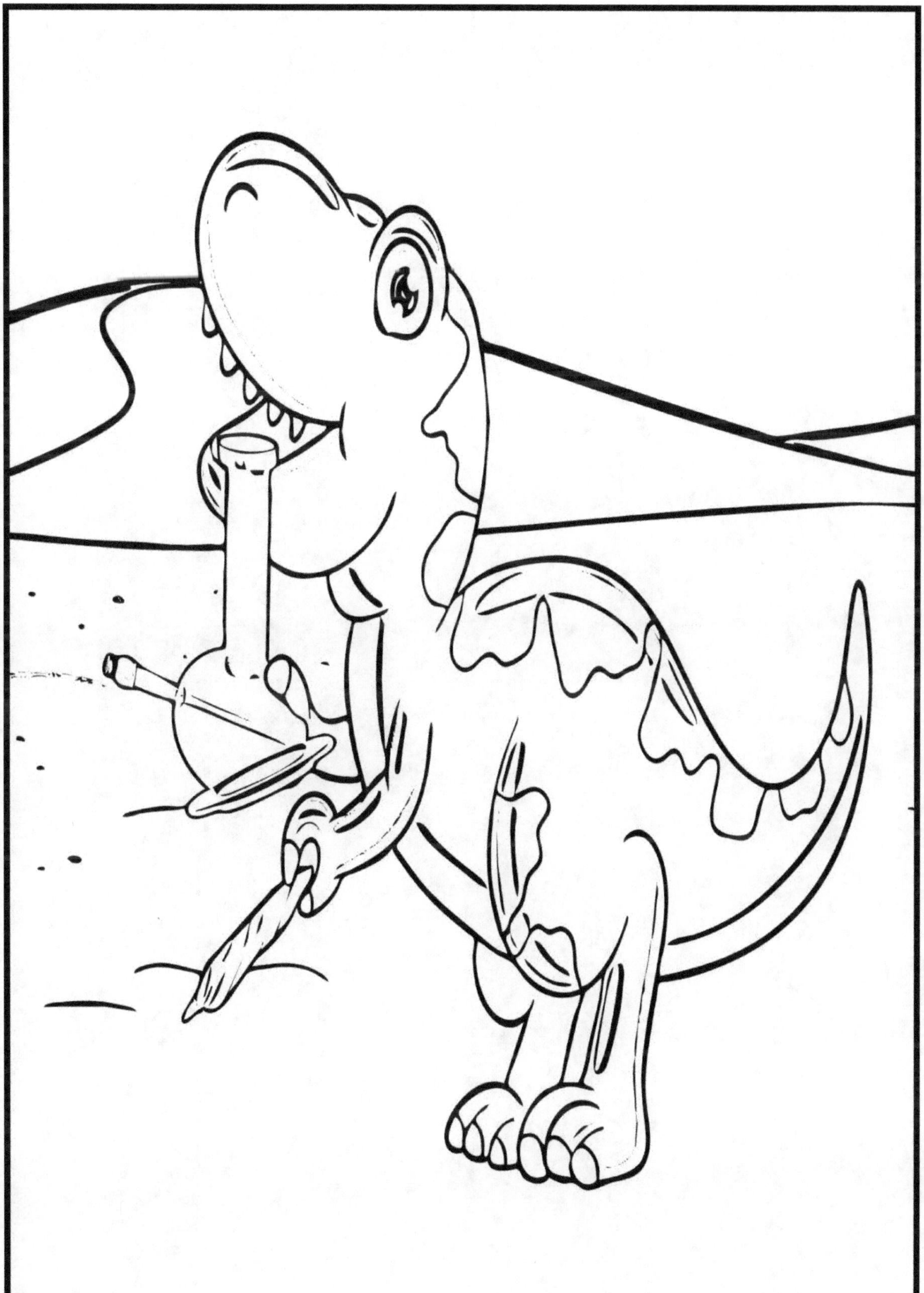

www.ingramcontent.com/pod-product-compliance
Lightning Source LLC
Chambersburg PA
CBHW080609180526
45168CB00007B/2848
* 9 7 8 1 5 1 8 7 0 3 3 2 4 *